Tim, the Golden Lion Tamarin

Written by Maria Chrislip
Illustrated by Christina Wald

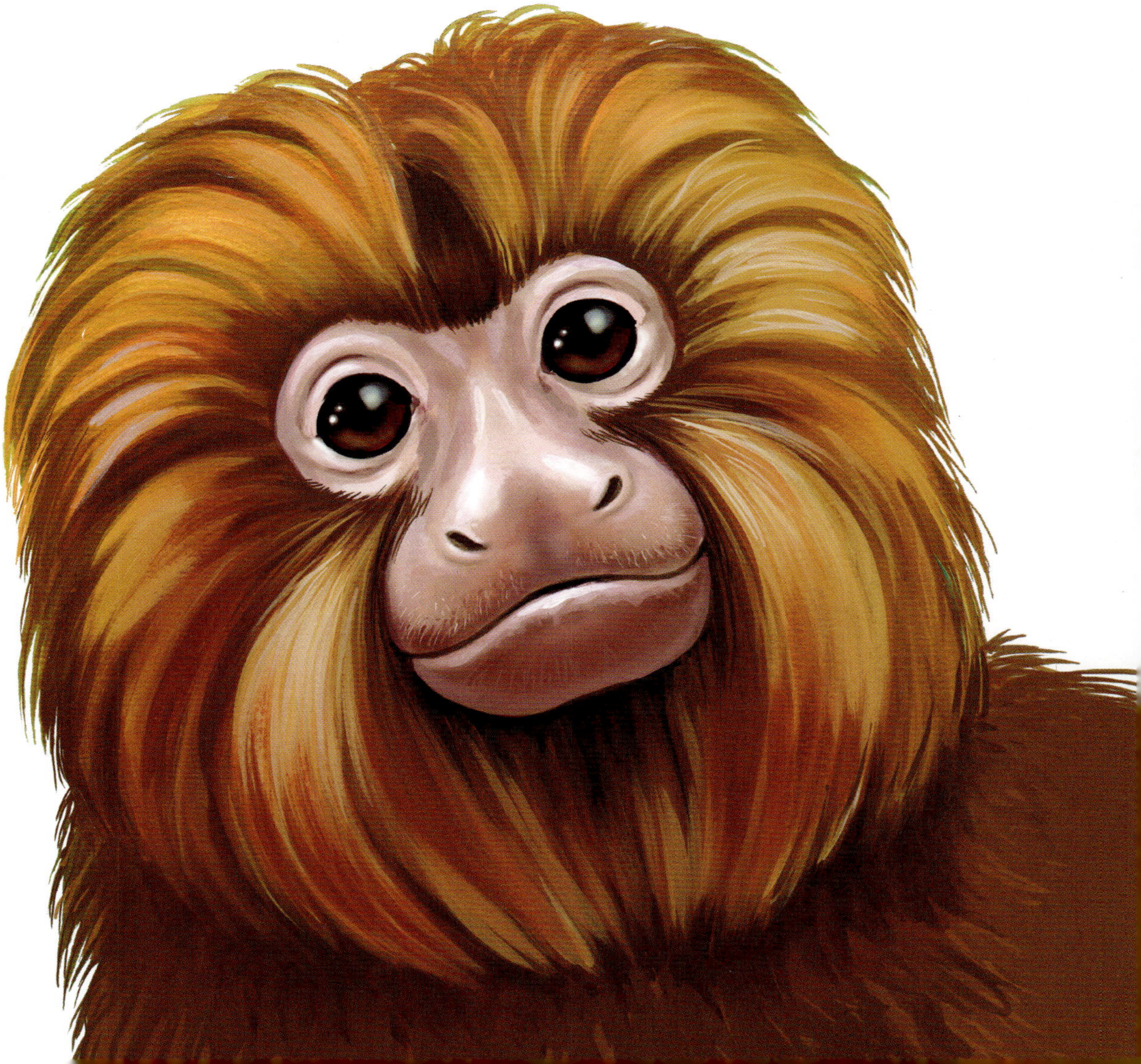

Welcome to my home. My name is Tim and I am a Golden Lion Tamarin. I live in the Atlantic forest of Brazil. It is a wet, warm, and beautiful coastal rain forest.

As you can see, I am quite good looking with all this golden fur around my face. I have been told that I look like a lion.

But, I am not king of the forest, and I don't even know how to roar. I am a little monkey who lives here with my Mama, Papa, older brother Pedro, and my twin brother Joe. Most Golden Lion Tamarins are twins.

When Joe and I were little babies we clung to our mother's back as she carried us around the forest. I could feel the hot sun beaming down on me. It is always hot in the rain forest.

When it was time to feed us her milk, my mother stopped under
the cool shade of a tree and sat on a large branch.

"It's time for milk," Mama said as she held us under her arms.

My father also carried us to the tallest trees and used his long fingers to grab the sweetest berries. With his claw-like nails he cut the berries into tiny pieces and carefully placed them in our hands. I could barely wait for my turn, and I would make a rasping noise as I tried to take the fruit from my brother.

"Be patient, Tim," Papa often whispered.

Now that I'm bigger, I spend most days with my brothers Joe and Pedro. Our parents keep an eye on us as we jump from tree to tree looking for sweet, juicy, round fruits.

"Ooh! There goes a hopping bug!" I screech to my brothers.

Katydid bugs are my favorite. I can catch more than anyone in the forest because I move very quickly.

But my favorite thing of all is nectar. I love how it drips through my fingers and gets all gooey and sticky. Yum!

After a long day in the forest I am very messy.

"It's time to get groomed," Papa calls to me.

I happily climb on his lap, and he lovingly licks me clean. With his long fingers Papa grooms my hair. It tickles my head, and I can't stop giggling.

"Stay still, Tim," Papa says, hugging me.

I sit as still as I can so he can finish combing my long golden mane. I want to look handsome for Mama.

As the sun sets, the forest becomes dark and a bit cooler. My home is covered with many beautiful green trees, orchids, and vines. I especially like to drink the water left on the colorful bromeliad plants and feel the mist on my mane from the gentle rain. I love my home.

But today I feel sad. The forest where I live is surrounded by cities which keep growing bigger and bigger. And so my home gets smaller and smaller.

"What's that?" I hear Papa make a loud piercing sound! The branches are shaking. He is calling to warn us of a stranger in our forest. Quickly, Mama, Joe, and I climb as fast as we can and hide in a hollow tree. I feel so scared!

My brother Pedro does not see us as he hides in another tree hole. The stranger cuts down his tree and Pedro jumps out before it crashes to the ground.

"Jump to me," Papa cries to Pedro.

Papa grabs Pedro and carries him back to our hole.

The forest is silent. Not a screech from the monkeys or a flap from the birds can be heard.

All the animals are scared. I am so sad and angry that I quickly take off on a long vine and call out through the forest.
I am as loud as the roar of a lion.

The other birds and animals hear my call and jump and call to each other in the forest. They know who I am—Tim, the Golden Lion Tamarin. I do not want to lose my home and my family. There are only a few of us left!

It has been a long day in the forest. Mama, Papa, Pedro, Joe, and I curl up together in our tree. Mama hugs me, and I feel safe again. I look up at the bright stars twinkling softly in the night sky. Together we pray to save our precious rain forest—the Atlantic forest I call my home.